P9-CRZ-929

GETTING TO KNOW THE WORLD'S GREATEST ARTISTS

MARY CASSATT

WRITTEN AND ILLUSTRATED BY MIKE VENEZIA

CONSULTANT SARA MOLLMAN UNDERHILL

Ⓟ CHILDRENS PRESS®
CHICAGO

For the special girls in my life,
Elizabeth, Laura, and Brigette

Cover: *Mother and Child.* c. 1890.
Oil on canvas, 35⅜ x 25⅜ inches.
Courtesy Wichita Art Museum, Wichita, Kansas.
The Roland P. Murdock Collection

Library of Congress Cataloging-in-Publication Data

Venezia, Mike.
    Mary Cassatt / written and illustrated by Mike Venezia
        p.   cm. — (Getting to know the world's greatest
artists)
    Summary: Briefly examines the life and work of the
American Impressionist painter, describing and giving
examples of her art.
    ISBN 0-516-02278-4
    1.   Cassatt, Mary, 1844-1926—Juvenile
literature.   2.   Painting, American.   3.   Painting,
Modern—United States.   4.   Art appreciation.
[1.   Cassatt, Mary, 1844-1926.   2.   Artists.]
I.   Title.   II.   Series.
ND237.C3V46   1989
759.13—dc20   90-2165
[B]   CIP
[92]   AC

Mary Cassatt was born in
Allegheny, Pennsylvania, in 1844.
She is known as a great American
artist, even though she spent most of
her life living and painting in France.

After the Bath. 1901. Pastel, 25¾ x 39¼ inches.
The Cleveland Museum of Art. Gift from J.H. Wade

Mary Cassatt loved families and children. Her paintings and pastels of mothers with their babies are among her most famous works.

Mother About to Wash Her Sleepy Child. 1880. Oil on canvas, 39½ x 25¼ inches.
Los Angeles County Museum of Art. Mrs. Fred Hathaway Bixby Bequest

When Mary was seven years old,
her family left America and moved to
Paris, France, for a couple of years.
Mr. and Mrs. Cassatt wanted their

children to see all the wonderful
sights while they lived in Paris. They
took their children to the great art
museums and galleries, where Mary
saw her first works of art.

A few years after the Cassatt family returned to America, Mary decided she wanted to be an artist. Not just any artist, but a serious artist. At first, Mary's father was very upset.

In the 1880s, people felt women weren't supposed to be artists. They thought women should only have very polite hobbies, become someone's wife, and stay home to raise their children.

It was one of the few times Mary and her father didn't get along.

Finally, after realizing how much Mary wanted to be an artist, her father agreed to send her to art school.

Mary studied very hard at the Pennsylvania Academy of the Fine Arts. After four years there, she decided a better way to learn about art would be to copy the paintings of the world's great artists.

There were very few paintings by
great artists in America at that time,
so in 1866 Mary Cassatt left for
France. She spent as much time as
she could in art museums, copying
famous paintings.

Mary Cassatt was becoming a pretty good artist. So she entered one of her paintings in the Paris Salon.

The Salon was an important place to have your paintings shown. People from all over the world came to look at—and maybe buy—the paintings they saw there.

It wasn't easy getting a painting into the Paris Salon. It was even harder if you were a woman artist, especially an *American* woman artist.

On the Balcony. 1873. Oil on canvas, 39¾ x 32½ inches.
Philadelphia Museum of Art. The W.P. Wilstach Collection

But in 1872, Mary's painting *On the Balcony* was accepted by the judges of the great Salon.

The Salon accepted four more of Mary Cassatt's paintings. Then something happened that changed Mary's life.

At that time, a small group of artists called Impressionists were painting in new and exciting ways.

They didn't like the rules the Salon had made about the way art should look. They didn't think the Salon's judges should decide what was good or bad about paintings either.

One of the Impressionists, Edgar Degas, asked Mary to join their group.

Mary was thrilled.

Mary had seen paintings done by the Impressionists. She loved the bright, beautiful colors that Claude Monet, Camille Pissarro, Auguste Renoir, and the other Impressionists used.

The Artist's Garden at Vetheuil.
1880. By Claude Monet,
oil on canvas, 59⅝ x 47⅝ inches.
National Gallery of Art, Washington.
Ailsa Mellon Bruce Collection

Boulevard des Italiens, Morning, Sunlight. 1897.
By Camille Pissarro,
oil on canvas, 28⅞ x 36¼ inches.
National Gallery of Art, Washington.
Chester Dale Collection

Right: *A Girl with a Watering Can.* 1876.
By Auguste Renoir,
oil on canvas, 38½ x 28¾ inches.
National Gallery of Art, Washington.
Chester Dale Collection

16

The Dancers. c. 1899. Pastel on paper, 24½ x 25½ inches.
The Toledo Museum of Art, Toledo, Ohio. Gift of Edward Drummond Libbey

But, most of all, Mary liked the work of Edgar Degas. She thought his colors, unusual angles, and the way he painted people made his paintings perfect.

La Jeune Mariée. c. 1875.
Oil on canvas,
34¾ x 27½ inches.
Collection of The
Montclair Art Museum. Gift of
the Max Kade Foundation

Mary Cassatt and Edgar Degas became close friends. Mary learned all she could from Degas. Soon she stopped using dark background colors and painting people in fancy costumes like in the painting above. She stopped doing things the judges at the Salon would have accepted.

Little Girl in a Blue Armchair. 1878. Oil on canvas, 35¼ x 51⅛ inches.
National Gallery of Art, Washington. Collection of Mr. and Mrs. Paul Mellon

She started to paint people as they
really looked, doing everyday things.
Her colors got brighter, too.

In the Omnibus (The Tramway).
1891. Drypoint, soft-ground
and aquatint printed in
color on three plates.
Mr. and Mrs. Martin A. Ryerson
Collection. Photograph © 1990,
The Art Institute of Chicago.

Mary kept working with Edgar
Degas. They experimented with
different types of art. For a while,
Mary made a series of special color
prints.

Women Admiring a Child. 1897. Pastel, 26 x 32 inches. © The Detroit Institute of Arts.
Gift of Edward Chandler Walker

They also experimented with pastels, mixing them with oil, turpentine, and even steam. They were trying to find ways to make the chalky colors as bright as possible and make the pastels sink deep into the paper.

In 1877, Mary's mother, father, and sister, Lydia, came to live with her in Paris. Her brothers and their families would visit Mary, too. Mary used the members of her family as models in many of her paintings and pastels.

Woman and Child Driving. 1881. Oil on canvas, 35¼ x 51½ inches.
Philadelphia Museum of Art. The W.P. Wilstach Collection

In the painting above, Mary
showed her sister, Lydia, driving a
carriage. Mary was interested in
photography and framed this
painting so the pony and carriage are
cut off. Mary knew that framing her
painting like a snapshot would give
more importance to her sister and the
little girl sitting next to her.

In 1892, Mary was very happy to receive an invitation from America. She was asked to make a huge painting, called a mural, for the Woman's Building at the Chicago World's Fair. The painting was so large that the canvas had to be lowered into a ditch while Mary was working on it so that she could reach the top!

Baby Reaching for an Apple.
1893. Oil on canvas,
39½ x 25¾ inches.
Virginia Museum of
Fine Arts, Richmond

The painting mysteriously disappeared after the fair. Some people think the smaller painting shown above may have been a study for Mary's huge painting.

Breakfast in Bed. 1897. Oil on canvas, 25⅝ x 29 inches. Henry E. Huntington
Library and Art Gallery, San Marino, California. The Virginia Steele Scott Collection

Mary Cassatt never had children of
her own, but she seemed to understand
the love between mothers and their
babies better than any other artist.

The Bath. 1891-1892. Oil on canvas, 39½ x 26 inches. Robert Waller Fund.
Photograph © 1988, The Art Institute of Chicago. All rights reserved.

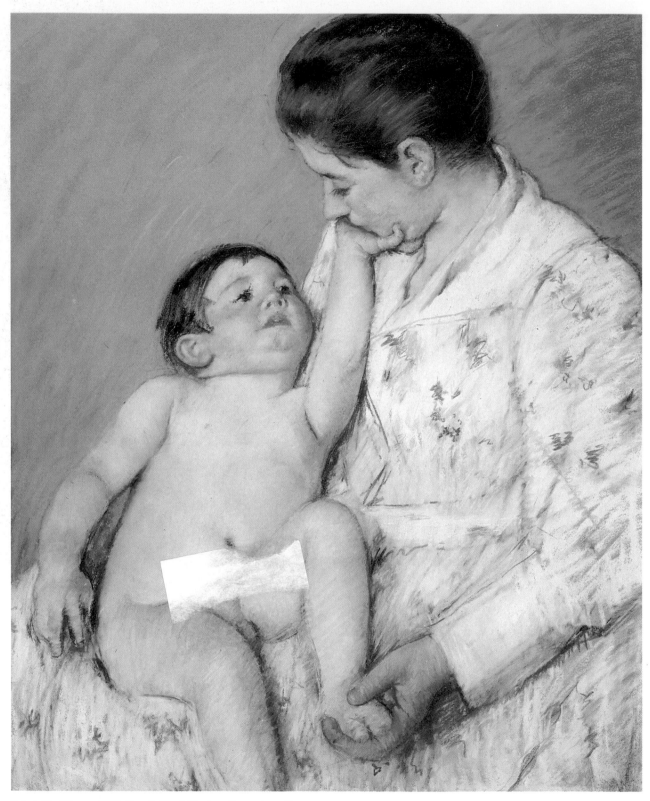

Baby's First Caress. 1891. Pastel, 30 x 24 inches. From the collection of the New Britain Museum of American Art, Connecticut. Harriet Russell Stanley Fund

The Boating Party. 1893-1894. Oil on canvas, 35½ x 46⅛ inches.
National Gallery of Art, Washington. Chester Dale Collection

Whether she used soft pastels or
strong shapes and bright colors, Mary
Cassatt's pictures are always warm
and friendly.

Mary Cassatt's paintings make you feel like you're right there, looking in on someone during a special moment.

Mother and Child. c. 1890. Oil on canvas, 35⅜ x 25⅜ inches. Courtesy Wichita Art Museum, Wichita, Kansas. The Roland P. Murdock Collection

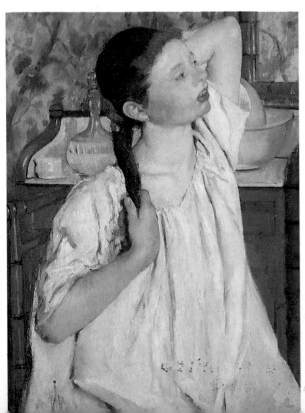

She made ordinary, everyday scenes important,

Girl Arranging Her Hair. 1886. Oil on canvas, 29½ x 24½ inches. National Gallery of Art, Washington. Chester Dale Collection

and helped make
the world realize
that women could
be great artists, too.

At the Theatre. 1879.
Pastel on paper, 21¹³/₁₆ x 18⅛ inches.
The Nelson-Atkins Museum of Art,
Kansas City, Missouri. Anonymous gift

Mary Cassatt
painted with love,
in a way few
artists have ever
been able to do.

Detail of *Breakfast in Bed* on page 26

It's fun to see real Mary Cassatt paintings. When you look closely, you'll be surprised at how she used little flecks of color to make eyes and noses, and to capture the delicate expressions on her people's faces.

The pictures in this book came from the museums listed below:

The Art Institute of Chicago, Chicago, Illinois
The Cleveland Museum of Art, Cleveland, Ohio
The Detroit Institute of Art, Detroit, Michigan
Henry E. Huntington Library and Art Gallery, San Marino, California
Los Angeles County Museum of Art, Los Angeles, California
Montclair Art Museum, Montclair, New Jersey
National Gallery of Art, Washington, D.C.
National Portrait Gallery, Washington, D.C.
The Nelson-Atkins Museum of Art, Kansas City, Missouri
New Britain Museum of American Art, New Britain, Connecticut
Philadelphia Museum of Art, Philadelphia, Pennsylvania
The Toledo Museum of Art, Toledo, Ohio
Virginia Museum of Fine Arts, Richmond, Virginia
Wichita Art Museum, Wichita, Kansas